XTREME FISHING

SALTWATER FISHING

BY S.L. HAMILTON

A&D Xtreme
An imprint of Abdo Publishing | www.abdopublishing.com

Visit us at
www.abdopublishing.com

Published by Abdo Publishing Company, a division of ABDO, PO Box 398166, Minneapolis, Minnesota 55439. Copyright ©2015 by Abdo Consulting Group, Inc. International copyrights reserved in all countries. No part of this book may be reproduced in any form without written permission from the publisher. A&D Xtreme™ is a trademark and logo of Abdo Publishing Company.

Printed in the United States of America, North Mankato, Minnesota.
102014
012015

Editor: John Hamilton
Graphic Design: John Hamilton
Cover Design: Sue Hamilton
Cover Photo: Thinkstock
Interior Photos: Alamy-pgs 8-9, 17, 22, 22-23, 26-27, 27, 28, 29; iStock-pgs 1, 2-3, 4-5, 6, 7, 8, 10-11, 12, 13, 14-15, 16, 18-19, 20, 21, 24-25, 30-31, 32.

Websites
To learn more about Fishing, visit booklinks.abdopublishing.com. These links are routinely monitored and updated to provide the most current information available.

Library of Congress Control Number: 2014944878

Cataloging-in-Publication Data

Hamilton, S.L.
  Saltwater fishing / S.L. Hamilton.
    p. cm. -- (Xtreme fishing)
  ISBN 978-1-62403-683-5 (lib. bdg.)
  Includes index.
  1. Saltwater fishing--Juvenile literature.   I. Title.
  799.16--dc23

2014944878

Contents

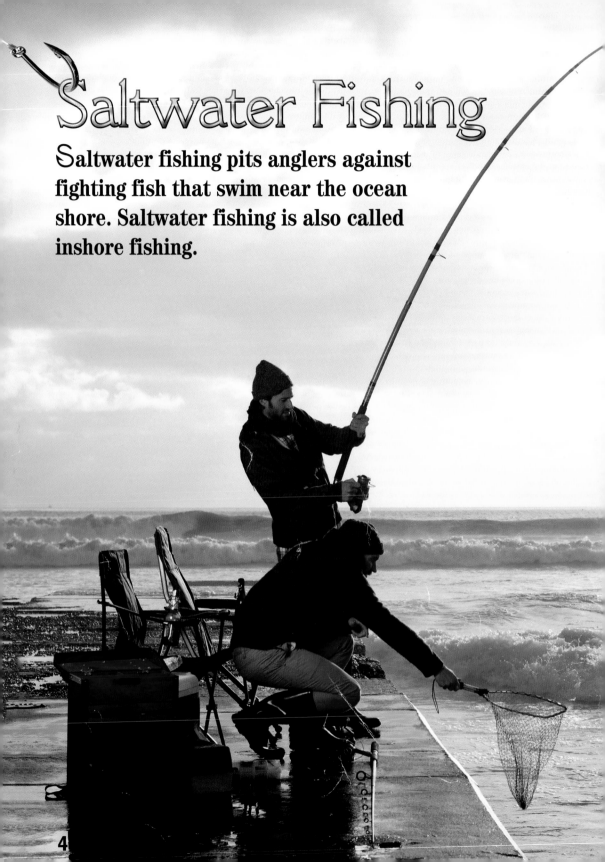

Saltwater Fishing

Saltwater fishing pits anglers against fighting fish that swim near the ocean shore. Saltwater fishing is also called inshore fishing.

Deep-sea fish are the biggest in the ocean. However, plenty of finned giants are found near the shore. It doesn't take a long boat ride to find them. Coastlines around the world offer sport fishermen a lot of excitement, and a chance to bring home a tasty prize.

Boats and Gear

Some anglers hunt for saltwater fish from a trolling boat. Others cast their hooks from beaches and docks. Light or medium tackle is usually enough to capture fish that swim in these waters.

Knowledge of each fish species is important for a good catch. Anglers study where fish live and what they eat. They choose their gear based on the kind of fish they hope to catch.

King Mackerel

The king mackerel is also called the kingfish. Anglers know they've hooked a big one when they see it swimming away in a burst of speed. Kingfish usually weigh from 5 to 35 pounds (2 to 16 kg). Some can grow to 100 pounds (45 kg). These powerful fish are found in the coastal waters of the western mid-Atlantic Ocean, the Gulf of Mexico, and as far south as Brazil, South America.

King mackerel often jump high in the air to attack lures or baitfish, such as balao and mullet. Most anglers catch kingfish while trolling, but others cast from piers.

XTREME FACT – Fishing contests are held for king mackerel by the Southern Kingfish Association. The SKA began in 1991 with 11 events. Today, the organization holds more than 50 events.

Great Barracuda

Great barracuda are a toothy fish that will happily snatch up another fish's intended meal. They are found in the warm waters of the Atlantic Ocean, the Gulf of Mexico, the Caribbean Sea, and the Red Sea. An average-sized barracuda grows up to 6 feet (1.8 m) long and weighs up to 20 pounds (9 kg). The largest ever caught weighed 84 pounds (38 kg).

Great barracuda bite on anything that looks like dinner, including live bait or lures. Once hooked, barracuda take off in long runs. In shallower waters, they will make great leaps into the air.

XTREME FACT– Barracuda are an oily fish. While edible, most people avoid eating them since barracuda have been traced to ciguatera poisoning. This food-borne illness is found in reef fish that consume toxins found in tropical waters. Barracuda eat the reef fish and multiply their chances of carrying the disease.

Sea Bass

Anglers love to hook sea bass on their lines. These fish are strong fighters. Some are named for their color, such as white, black, and striped. These are found in the waters around North America. European sea bass are found in the waters near Europe's coasts. To catch sea bass, anglers use lures and small baitfish, including squid and crustaceans. Sea bass are found near sandy bottoms and around kelp beds.

Snook

Snook are found only in coastal waters from Florida to Central America. They stay near mangrove estuaries, lagoons, and inlets. Anglers attract snook with live bait, such as pinfish, squirrelfish, shrimp, or mullet. They may also use flies. Bait is reeled in with a jerky motion. This makes it seem as if the snook's lunch is trying to escape.

When a snook is hooked, it leaps out of the water. These fish will try to tangle fishing lines around nearby obstacles, such as mangrove roots. Anglers must reel in the snook quickly. Otherwise, it will find a way to break the line and escape.

XTREME FACT – Snook may live in saltwater or freshwater. Fly fishermen may also go after snook.

Halibut

Halibut are the largest flatfish in the world. They are found along northern coastlines of the Atlantic and Pacific Oceans. They will eat almost anything. Halibut usually range in size from 50 to 150 pounds (23 to 68 kg). Some may grow up to 500 pounds (227 kg). Although they live near coastlines, halibut like deep water. Some are caught in water more than 3,500 feet (1,067 m) below the surface.

To catch halibut, anglers use lures or live bait, such as herring. Heavy sinkers drop the bait to the bottom of very deep water. Strong line is needed to bring the halibut up. Landing these monster-sized fish is a challenge. Most people agree it is one of the tastiest fish to eat.

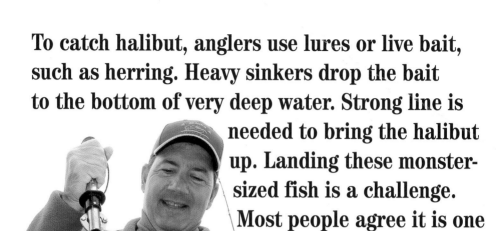

Grouper

Grouper are found worldwide. Many swim in the Gulf of Mexico. Although slow-growing, they become monster-sized fish. They may weigh 220 pounds (100 kg) or more!

Grouper rest near the sea floor. Fishermen drop down live bait, such as pinfish or mackerel. Or they may use weighted lures. They get a grouper's attention by "jigging" the line, jerking it up and down. When a grouper bites, an angler has a powerful, stubborn fish on the line. If anglers can lift the fish at least 12 feet (3.7 m) off the ocean floor, they will probably succeed in pulling it all the way to the surface.

Salmon

King salmon and silver salmon are a tasty catch. They are found in the Pacific Ocean. They range from California to Alaska. Anglers hunt for salmon in the open ocean. Salmon are also found in bays, sounds, and near coastal rivers. They can swim into freshwater to eat and spawn. King salmon weigh 10 to 25 pounds (5 to 11 kg). Silver salmon weigh 6 to 12 pounds (3 to 5 kg).

Anglers troll for salmon using hooks baited with herring, sardine, and anchovy. Spoons and spinners also attract salmon. Sinkers are used to drop lines down deep, where the fish are feeding. Once hooked, salmon fight and jump. They are an exciting catch.

XTREME FACT– King salmon are also called chinook salmon. Silver salmon are also called coho salmon.

Cobia

In North America, cobia are found along the mid-Atlantic coast, and as far south as Florida. They also live along the coast of the Gulf of Mexico and in the Caribbean Sea. They often lurk near beaches or fixed objects, such as buoys and channel markers. Anglers hunt for them from boats, and by casting from beaches. Cobia usually reach sizes of 5 to 25 pounds (2 to 11 kg). They can get as big as 100 pounds (45 kg).

Streamlined cobia are powerful fighters and fast swimmers. They are caught using live bait, such as crabs, shrimp, mullet, and pinfish. Often, when one fish is hooked, the rest of the school will surface with it. Cobia are considered excellent fish to eat.

XTREME FACT – A cobia's dorsal fin resembles a shark's, but the fish are not related.

Red Snapper

Red snappers are an extremely popular catch. They are found off the coast of the United States from North Carolina to Texas. These brightly colored fish range in size from about 8 to 20 pounds (3.6 to 9 kg).

Some are found near the shore in 50 to 60 feet (15 to 18 m) of water, but today most swim in deeper waters. Fishermen go after red snappers with live bait or squid. Once hooked, these fish are fighters. They use strong head-shaking moves to try to throw the hook. A catch means a delicious meal for the angler.

XTREME FACT – Red snappers have been overfished. Since they are slow-growing fish, it takes several years for the population to rebound. Fishermen must check local regulations to find out how many they may catch.

Bluefish

Bluefish will bite on just about anything. If a school of bluefish encounters a school of mullet, menhaden, or herring, the blues go into an eating frenzy. Sharp-toothed blues will bite and gorge themselves on fish after fish, sometimes even turning the water red.

Bluefish rarely grow larger than 20 pounds (9 kg). Anglers chum the water with ground menhaden to draw in bluefish. They will troll with spoons, feathers, swimming plugs, and leadhead jigs. The sharp teeth of a blue can bite through standard monofilament line, so fishermen use stainless steel leaders. Once hooked, bluefish fight hard. When reeled in, anglers must be careful not to be bitten.

XTREME FACT – With a mouthful of sharp teeth and an aggressive attitude, bluefish are nicknamed the "piranha of the seas."

Dangers

Saltwater fishing has its own set of dangers. The weather can change quickly. Rough seas or a damaged boat or motor are all possible. Lightning strikes can occur, whether the angler is on a boat or on shore. Keeping a wary eye on the weather is vital for any fisherman.

No matter how experienced the angler, getting impaled by a fishhook is always possible. Hooks are usually unclean. Left untreated, a wound from a hook can easily become infected. It's important to let doctors remove the hook and disinfect the wound. Staying focused when casting, attaching lures or bait, and safely unhooking a fish are important.

Glossary

BAITFISH

Smaller fish on which game fish regularly feed. Baitfish are used to bait hooks.

CHUM

Bait consisting of blood and fish parts that is thrown into the water to attract game fish.

DORSAL FIN

The fin that is located on the top of a fish's back. On a shark, for example, the dorsal fin is the one that sticks out of the water when the shark is swimming near the surface.

JIG

A type of fishing lure. Jigs are lead sinkers with hooks built in, and covered with a colorful body to attract fish. Fishermen move jigs in a jerky, up-and-down motion to coax fish into biting the lure.

LEADER

A short length of material, such as nylon monofilament or stainless steel, that is used to attach hooks and lures to fishing line. Leaders are thicker and stronger than fishing line, which helps prevent the game fish from biting through the line. The thicker the leader, however, the easier it is for the game fish to see it and avoid the lure.

Sport Fish

A fish that anglers hunt because of its fierceness and difficulty in landing, making its capture an exciting sport.

Stainless Steel

A type of metal that is strong and resists rusting. Leaders are sometimes made of stainless steel.

Streamlined

The shape of a creature or object that reduces the drag, or resistance, of air or water flowing across its surface. This increases speed and ease of movement. Certain fish, such as barracuda and cobia, have a streamlined shape that allows them to swim faster because they don't have to push as hard to move through the water.

Tackle

Equipment used by fishermen, such as rods, reels, hooks, lines, and sinkers. Tackle is often kept in a tackle box.

Troll

To fish by trailing a baited hook and line behind a moving boat.

Index